Raw Thoughts

Swirling

in a Pot of Sugar

Alexandria Romei

DEDICATION

This book is for humans. Humans that feel and think and want to be seen and connect with others. This book is for the loud and outspoken, the quiet and analytical, and the one's finding their voice. This book is for those seeking inspiration to think in new ways or write poetry of their own. This book is for artists who want stories of inspiration for their drawings, paintings, and other masterpieces. This book is for those who are in dark spaces to know someone else has sat in those same places. This book is for the hopeless who are ready to give up. This book is for all humans to know that they are seen and heard and loved and can change the world. This book is for you to see the creative beauty inside of yourself and maybe just maybe, share it with the world as well.

Table of Contents

Body scars
Naked Invasion
Her Baby Hands Will Heal Me
When Sorry Got Old
My Morning Bourbon
If My Body Was a Crime Scene
Slingshot
The Mask You Wear

Daddy, dad, father, dead
I Think My Dad Loved Me?
About My Dad…
When My Dad Tried to Kidnap Me
Where Did My Dad Go?
I Choose
When Your Daddy Kills Himself
Where Was My Daddy Before?

Processing death
I'll Cross the Bridge
The story of Casper and Oli
Tick Tock
Hear Me Cry

Finding me
Who Am I
I Want to Walk Without Shoes Today
Words I Don't Own
I Walked the Blue, I Walked the Red
Where Do I Address My Prayers?
I'll Try to Practice What I Preach
392 Word Poem
The Gift to Sing
Maybe I'm the Quiet One
The Best and the Worst Don't Want to Share
Verbal Filter Glow up

Now it's Romei
Re: Your Father
Struggle with My Shape
Searching for the Me I Used to Be

Water, Waves, and Wonder
Dreams
Dancing Underwater
The Boat Sailed Across the Waterway
The Secret Doorway
I Gave My Stories to a Sailor

Love
I Gazed into Their Eyes
Little Luv Story
Broken Love, Healed Me Though
Whichever Way for You
Trust Me Now
The Sky in Your Eyes
When Love Explodes
Rainbow Vision
Love Her
Wild, Unapologetic Girl

Higher Than This World
Concrete Jungle #1
Concrete Jungle #2
Don't Break the Ice
Not Being Good Enough
My Ghost is Gone
Mania
Our Song
One Last Day
I Look to the Stars for Answers
Crazy
Burnt Disguise

Crazy Lady
What a Time in My Mind
Flower with Power

Redemption
Dear Voice in My Head
Shine on Me
Can't Call It Defeat
Just Tired
Remember Me
It Didn't End, so Here It Begins
I Send My Judgements Down to the River
Treasures to Re-Remember
Impossible Things I Do Everyday
Run Faster Towards the Life You're Running For

Loss comes in many forms
The Earth Is Dying…
The War Line
Baby Hat
Privilege

Illumination
I Am Here
To Be in the Light
Yoga
Young Girls Will Change the World
The World Is at My Fingertips
To Fly
A World of Connotations
I Like the Stars
Illumination Short Poems
Mixed Emotions
Wounded Hearts
Not Sure Which World I'm Living in
Out of Madness Comes Treasure

Preface

Some of my poems will reflect religious ideas. I have a Christian-based upbringing and attended Sunday school and Christian summer camps for many years, so Bible stories and the idea of God and Jesus are very familiar to me. Where I stand right now in life, I would not label myself with any religion. I believe in a higher power and love and I find value in ideas from multiple religions.

Another note is that some of my poems are written from my own point of view, they reflect certain things I have experienced or thoughts I have. Other poems are written in first person, yet do not reflect things that have happened to me. For example, I've never been physically abused or gotten pregnant. So, when you come across those sorts of poems, just know they reflect me processing other people's stories or experiences or what I imagine those things must feel like. Also, some poems are my point of view at that time; I would not necessarily write them again because my views have changed or new information is available to me that I was unaware of before.

My hope is that these poems will make you laugh, cry, think deeper, or feel like you can relate. Enjoy!

Intro Poems

Humans. Create. Poetry.

Humankind spread their words around
Glue them together
Like a puzzle but better
Let imagery and consonance form
Until poetry is born

February 2019

My Poems are Ready Now

I've written these poems before
Filled many pages with anger, love and way more
But only in the safety of my own head
Never out loud or in writing
Too scared of the nakedness of my own thoughts
I lugged around all this dusty armor
But now I'm ready to shed
Ready to spread
All these traumas, mysteries, and incomplete stories
I hope each one makes you feel something new
Or gives you a chance to smile and whisper "me too"

March 2019

You're Reading my Poem

Somehow or another I've grasped your attention
You're reading these words
That I once sat by myself and wrote
There is a tension in the energy between us
I feel you reading them
Each one with a curiosity
A curiosity that I once experienced
When the words first whispered to me
From the wonders of my own head

March 2019

Raw Thoughts Swirling in a Pot of Sugar

Sugar makes my dreams crazy
But the only three other words that rhyme with
Crazy
Are
Daisy
Lazy and
Lastly, hazy
Daisy:
noun: any number of numerous composite plants having
flower heads with well-developed ray flowers usually
arranged in a single whirl
"Well developed flower rays" sounds sweet to my soul
When I was born
At 10 seconds old
I was given the middle name Ray
And though it's from my grandpa, the definition is
"spread from or as if from a central point"
"As if"
Well this can pretty much explain my idea process
See I have these brilliant thoughts
And when I go about explaining them
They spread out like a rainbow
The thoughts are connected but not on the same playing
field
Some are up in the sky
While others are trying to stay grounded
Not trying to fly
See, sugar is an addicting drug
Making my mind fly high
And my thoughts rapidly quantify
I truly try to look at my problems with a logical eye
A sense of reasoning

But as I said
My middle name is Ray
And the dictionary's sentence example is
"delicate lines rayed out at each corner of her eyes"
Imagine yourself staring at two opposite corners of a room
looking for tiny, delicate lines
See, my family doesn't have to imagine
Because I tell them every time I have a new idea

February 2018

Alexandria Romei

Systems, Meds, and Suicide

Invasions

It's been a year now
I'm doing so good
they were so proud of me
when the doctor told me how long
I had left
they said it's all paying off
all the dedication
and frustration
it was all part of the
original equation
their invasion on my brain
and my patience put to waste
it's all been for this special occasion
they said they had a confession
that it would probably cause me
depression
but does that even matter when we
have reached this level of
obsession
my last observation was of my
voices of obsession making a
confession
telling me that my brain
has been taken
my knowledge has been shaven
it has all been replaced with
limitations and presentations of
unrealistic expectations
they warned me that they did not
know of my soon-to-be
new destination
but they were so sweet
they wished me the best
and apologized for their invasion
As I left, they whispered one last thing,
"Don't worry, we're off to make new
"creations""

November 2016

Not Your Fault

You've been through a lot
You've been hit
You've been raped
You thought you'd never escape
But now you're out
And all grown up
Doing what's
Been done to you
But this will never be your fault
Because after all
How did it start

September 2016

Foster Kid

She was only eight years old
When she was told
She was being given up
For the seventh time
The first time was at birth
Her momma was too busy committing her next crime
No way she could raise
This little baby
Or the twelve she's had before
Now little Amaya was on her own
Again, In the foster system
"Social worker" she said
"When will I have any choices?"
"Oh, little Amaya, you'll have to wait till you're grown"
It doesn't matter how good you are
It doesn't matter how bad you want a place to call home
But your black skin and unfortunate genes
Have given you such a disadvantage
In this large evil world
Baby girl there's nothing I can do
She fights back tears as she stares into her social worker's eyes
A stuffed elephant from her birth daddy in one hand
And a trash bag full of hand me downs, a couple notebooks, and
one little dolly
In the other hand
She swallows her hope
As she tries to accept the fact that this is her childhood
That she'll always be misunderstood
Eventually there will be hope
But right now, she must go rest her little head on a stranger's
pillow
And dream about the day she can finally say she's loved

November 2017

The Mission to Celebrate Every Life

Suicide literally goes
against every single one of
our deepest instincts
yet look at the statistics
suicide is on the rise
and this brings tears to my eyes
for every suicide there are
25 attempts
and how is this ok
why are we allowing
our loved ones
to go down this road
over three million teens have
experienced a depressive episode
and the cause of this we
do not fully know
the logic is non-existent
but the hurt and pain
are more real than ever
spreading awareness is good
but reaching out to those
around you is even better
we must put down
our phones
and make some conversation
we are living in America
with people dying for our freedom
let's act like a United Nation
the boy you saw on the street
earlier, his body may now
be in cremation
these are not
depressing facts
this is our truth
this is our truth right now
but not forever
as I hope to inspire people
to create connection

to take breaks from
the addiction
of our rectangles
of constant stimulation
those around us
are struggling
some in silence
and some in blood
we all have the power to
reach out and help someone
to stop their suicide contemplation
the top cause to someone's
suicide is family problems
something that we all can
be there to support each other with
on average there are 123 suicides
per day just in America and in my
opinion, suicide is the most unnatural
way to die
changing the world and
lowering the rates of
suicide
will take a combination
of determination
and constant demonstration
of love
but I believe we all
can do it
this world and every
single person on it
is a beautiful creation
every life deserves
a celebration

August 2018

I Die, You Win

I hit, you punch
I yell, you scream
I push, you shove
I steal, you rob
I cut, you kill
I die, you win

May 2016

Sorry to Annoy You So Much, My Head Just Really Hurts

Stop screaming so loud
Stop kicking the furniture
Start sitting over there in that chair
Start cutting up your wrists
Stop yelling at us
Stop pleading on and on
Start crying in your room
Start swallowing those pills

May 2016

What It Took for You to Be Named

You were never given a name
That made you sad
Which turned to mad
Now you're locked up
But you have a name
Oh my gosh
What did it take

May 2016

Activities of the Prisoners

You'll never guess
What I did today
I slit my wrists
I took some pills
I skipped a meal
And drilled some holes
It felt so real
I felt so dead
Lying here in my bed
But you see
Being locked in here
Makes this all a dream

May 2016

The Death Sentence vs The Life Sentence

A capital crime
Gets you a death sentence
Which means you don't pay the time
Maybe a felony
Is a more serious crime
Because with that
You pay the time
You pay each living day
So next time you're in court
Think real well
Because with a felony
Only time will tell

May 2016

Unfair Systems

Systems everywhere
Supposedly keeping things fair
But when he rapes, kills, and wins
And you steal, lie, and lose
Maybe you will start to think and care
But it won't matter because you'll be caged
They'll say it's loss protection
But it's really a projection
Of the systems being unfair

May 2016

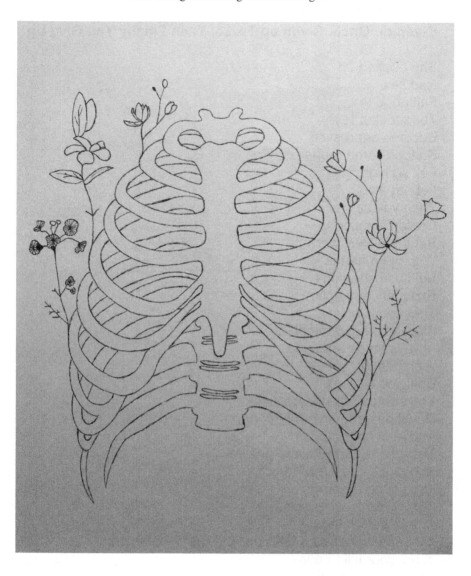

Given up Once, Given up Twice, Then Finally You Give Up

She hooked up
Had sex
Felt good
Then took a test
Became depressed
So took some drugs
Felt so high
Let out a cry
Then you came
Couldn't function
But there they were
With open hands
Said you shouldn't
Experience rejection
They took you in
Kissed you goodnight
Always made sure you
Were alright
Until you weren't
You started asking questions
Questions about your birth parents
And heaven
They didn't know how to answer
You didn't know how to cope
Too young for drugs
But you took some pills,
screamed too loud,
ruined too much furniture, and left them wondering
about your little future
Sent to the hospital
They signed the papers
To give you up
Now you're an orphan
Being held to the floor
And all we think is
Why does this even happen anymore

May 2016

Adoption Would Have Been the Loving Thing to Do

They say you're a mistake
A lack of protection
But if they didn't want you
From the start
They should have made it clear
Because now you're in the bathroom
And will never shed another tear

May 2016

Just Fix Me with Meds

Medicate me
Give me drugs
Shut me up
No
Shut me down
Make it easy
Make it quick
Numb the pain
So you feel sane
I'll finally be quiet
You'll finally be happy

April 2017

Hospital Overwhelm

Doctors, psychiatrists, nurses
Only feels like armed forces
All running towards me
Chanting time to get healthy
Contained to a room with only a bed
Every hour taking a different med
Channel surfing
Monsters cursing
All I can see is my IV
The rest just seems so blurry
Let's send her here
Let's send her there
I don't really even care
Get me out
I'm gonna shout
Say to go away
Save the "fun" for another day

July 2016

9 Medications and a Monkey

I shove eight of them down my throat
With half a glass of water
Any more would make me bloat
Yesterday it was nine
But my mom didn't pick up
My prescription
Sometimes it just feels too long
To wait in the line
And now she's out of town
So today it's only eight
My doctor, he says he doesn't
Want me to frown
So, there's one for depression
If I'm feeling down
Which I feel everyday
And there's one for bipolar
For when I feel every which way
Which I definitely feel today
Unless today is yesterday
But yesterday has already passed
And it's definitely not tomorrow
No no I know it's today, right?
See, there's one for my memory
It helps my thinking to not be so blurry
I think it works
And there's one for my anger
Because of all my pent-up fury
Because I'm mad of the amount of medication
The doctors put in cute orange bottles and force down my throat
I feel like I need some mental vacation
Away from the talking
In therapy I'm learning the blocking
The blocking of my thoughts
My thoughts are bad they say, so I can't listen to them
I block them and make them go away

See it's a brilliant tool
But it causes me anxiety
So, I take an anti-anxiety medication
And then they thought I had anorexia
When I didn't eat for two months
So, I have an OCD pill
But it turns out my anxiety medicine just
Makes me not hungry
So of course, there's another pill that raises the bill
As well as my appetite
I don't know why I still take an OCD medication when I've been undiagnosed with the
OCD diagnosis
But they say the side effects of coming off could cause me mental stress
Hahahahaha
Doctors are smart.
So, now I've told you about
Seven of my pills
I think I forgot the eighth one...
No no no
I have it
It's back in my head
It's for hallucinations
At least that's what the monkey just told me
Can you see the monkey?
That's why the doctor says
I'm in therapy
In the therapy room, the monkey turns blue
And on the days the monkey is grey
I look at it, and then in mirror
And I say me too me too
We're both grey today
Me in my heart
But you, you've dressed the part
So, if you're curious what the
Ninth medication is

The one that I should be taking
Well I can just tell you now
That's my depression medicine
And my obsession medicine
Don't exactly agree
They cause hallucinations
And make me not hungry
So I have a pill that helps with that
It's supposed to make it the opposite
Doctor J says I need two of those magic hallucination curing
opposite pills to have an effect
But my mother's checkbook says differently
So I only take one
My thinking may be a bit blurry
But at least I'm getting half the help I need, right?
I actually talked to my doctor this morning
He says I'm just stressed out
And we're gonna raise my anxiety medication tomorrow
And after that, everything should be okay he says
And my therapist says to trust the doctor
And my doctor says to trust the therapist
So I think I'll be okay
At least, that's what the monkey says

September 2017

Being Depressed at a Coffee Shop

Being Depressed at a Coffee Shop

It's sad in here
It's dark in here
I want to BE back, not GO back
The music is sad
The fireplace is on yet we're NOT a family
Why is the fireplace on when we're not a family

November 2017

Depressed Interpretations

The music just stopped
Started again
This song is a bit happier I guess

November 2017

Raw Frustration

I feel mad
Like how I get mad at my mom
In my own home
I usually suppress everything
But right now
I want to cry
I want to throw things
Tell people to shut up
Cry some more
Punch something
Think about suicide
Cry some more
But instead I'm writing
It's not as satisfying
But at least no one else has to
Feel my pain

November 2017

Evening Coffee Shop Thoughts

I don't like it here
But I'm becoming a bit more comfortable
I hope he knows her
Or that's creepy
Turn the music down
The baby is being loud
It's ok to be unsure of your degree
The fire isn't even that big
The woman is carrying a very big bag
Being lazy isn't good in this world
Shake hands when you meet people
It's always good
Don't say crazy lady
Never say crazy lady
Glasses are nice
You can make fire with them
And see with them
Help people
That's always good
Enrich yourself
The baby left now
I'm still hungry
When you see people a lot, introduce yourself
Standing next to the fire makes you warm but standing in the
fire makes you hot!
Green jackets are in season right now
Green jackets are worn in the military
It's always good to say thank you
It's always good to take advantage of opportunities
Don't say no
When they talk loudly it hurts
Art is cool
Create some

November 2017

I Feel the Need to Draw

I feel the need to draw and fill something in
Probably because I feel empty inside
Just a bit of shading will do
That's ok.
But I'm not

November 2017

Body Scars

Naked Invasion

there was no asking
no eye contact
not even persuasion
he just pushed down my shoulders
and restricted my breathing
his large build
to my small figure
was no equal equation
he whispered "happy birthday to me"
said it was his
"special occasion"
he peeled off my clothes
rubbed his saliva on my
cheeks
and then started *the invasion*
something was inside of me
it looked like a large, evil raisin
I felt out of place
I couldn't determine my location
I didn't breathe for a moment or two
then I had a heart palpitation
my whole being started to experience
helpless anger and inflammation
he looked at my naked body
with fascination
the puke rose to my mouth
and then came the hallucination
so I escaped into my imagination
I guess I'd rather think about ghosts
then be in reality to experience
a naked invasion

January 2019

Her Baby Hands Will Heal Me

The bright red blood drips below me
Drip drop drip drop
Providing evidence of a baby
Fresh out of a mother's womb

It haunts me
What have I done
The beauty in my hands captures me
But I can't forget the loss of the first one
How she was ripped out of me
Because I made a mistake
And then another mistake for losing her
But this beauty
The beauty in my hands
Takes. My. Breath. Away.

Maybe she is my first one, placed back in my womb to give me
a second chance
It's hard to imagine that she could have had a sister, but now
she never will

I didn't know it would be this hard
I didn't know it would be this beautiful
I didn't know she would be this beautiful
I didn't know blood could be this beautiful
I didn't know the pain would go away as soon as our eyes
locked

That her baby hands would slowly heal my heart, my hands,
my soul

What a gift she is
What a journey I have ahead of me

June 2017

When Sorry Got Old

When sorry got old
I would punch and hit
Lie that I got bit
Steal and sneak
My thoughts made me feel like a freak
Mom would roll her eyes to some of the shit that I would speak
Sister would cry and sit against her bedroom door to keep me
away, to avoid the pain I was waiting to deliver
I would feel exploding jealousy and always wish that I had more
No one could relate to me
And that's all I really craved
I searched high and low
Yet no one just like me
So again, I misbehaved
Tried to resist the temptations
But finally, I caved
My mind lost control of my arm as I swung it towards my sister
My hand became a fist as I expressed why I felt pissed
Out of jealousy, annoyance or sadness. Doesn't really matter
why. Just matters that I did it and could never take it back.
I begged her not to tattletale
I wanted to be her friend
It felt like my mind was in jail
Restricted, out of control and constantly being punished yet still
innocent and malleable
Sorry, sis. I'm sorry. Please don't tell. Please be my friend.
I begged over and over again.
Finally she said "sorry is old."
It's lost its power.
This is when my mind collapsed like a leaning tower
This is when the abuse transformed from being expressive and
external
To being passive, sneaky, sly and internal

December 2018

This poem is really hard for me to out there because it feels very personal and I'm afraid of people judging me. This poem is raw, vulnerable, written without a filter and unedited. I wasn't going to include it in my book. But then I realized that's some of the best type of poetry. The type you're afraid to share.

My Morning Bourbon

I've come to appreciate the taste of my morning bourbon
Flooding my glass of cold milk
Soaking up the stress from yesterday
As it trickles down
My bladed throat
Finally
Making it soft
So my words can flow
So I can talk
So I can scream
So I can whisper
Without the swords
Of my throat
Hitting my loved ones
This is why I drink
My morning bourbon
In a glass of cold milk
This is why my morning bourbon
Had never failed me

June 2017

If My Body Was a Crime Scene

You would look at my eyes
And know it was a car accident
Because everything is happening so quickly
Impulse
Impulse
Impulse
I'm sorry
I didn't mean to hit you
But now I've been hit
And I forgot that I hurt you
I'm so sorry
You would look at my heart
And know it was a hit and run
I felt so bad
Impulse
Impulse
Impulse
I sped away
My thoughts were racing
The police were pacing
Trying to figure out
Where I went
Chasing me down
As quick as they can
You would look at my breasts
And you would see the case files of the culprit
So large
But I don't like to show them
I keep them hidden
Hope they'll shrink
Or even disappear
Because I didn't always have them
And I thought they were cool at first

Ya know like just one small charge
A night or two in jail
Makes me look a little tough
Not too bad though
But they keep getting bigger
More evidence is found
More crimes to be convicted of
You would look at my legs at my legs
And know the runaway car
Was loud and fast
Strong
And capable
Yet at its best
Just an accessory
Because when a car is doing what it loves most
It's the driver that matters
The arms and core
That carry
But the engine powers it all
My calves purely muscle
The tires made of steel
My thighs are thick and strong
The engine is large and powerful
That's why the car is getting away so quickly
You would look at my arms and know
There was a rainbow license plate
And a couple of
Bow and arrows in the back of the car
Which you wish you didn't see them
Because it just complicates the case
You would look at my waist
Blood Type S
Capital S
For stretch marks
Long and red

Some faded
Some new
But this wouldn't be too helpful
You see it too often
But the new detective by your side
Would point them out five times over and over again
She's never seen them in the mirror
But you've seen them
Seen them red
Blue
Bright
Faded
They come as no shock
But you take note anyways
Capital S
For stretch marks
You tell the young detective
You'll see them someday
And then you'll see them over and over again
Eventually they will be no surprise
You say
You would look at my back
And see the trail of which the cars we're driving on
The long map
Of a normal day
To a crime scene
It wasn't meant to happen
You study it
How did that car move five lanes so quickly
No way you exclaim
Ask for a reprint
Go ahead
It's the same thing
The same map
No mistakes were made

You shake your head
The car was never dented
But now it's scratched and burned
Why, why did it happen
Impulse
Impulse
Impulse
That's the reason
You look at my armpits
No evidence there
It's useless
No hair was ever grown
Oh that's new you say
It's true it's true
It's just new to you
But it's different
So it's frightening
You investigate
The lack of evidence
Drives you crazy
The lack of evidence
Itself
Is no evidence
Leave it alone
The car was made that way
Always running on adrenaline
The thoughts running through the veins of my body
Keep me warm enough
Excess hair is not needed
But my head it is blessed
You look at my hair
What a responsible car owner
You exclaim
Beautiful paint job
Shiny windows

Sparkling clean mirrors
It all frames the car so well
Makes it look so innocent
It makes it harder to solve the case
Because you are deceived by one small feature
How could I be blessed with thick golden, perfectly curly hair
I ask every night
I recognize my blessings
Don't get me wrong
But when one thing happens
It's
Just
Impulse
Impulse
Impulse
And now you're looking at my body
As if it was a crime scene

July 2017

Slingshot

Let me tell you how happy I am
Everyone is out to get me
Maybe I'll live forever
But today I'm going to die

You walk in the door and I want to scream
You're really amazing, I'm glad we're a team

I have these shades, they are very dark, they are super glued
to my face
Make me a promise and they'll fall off,
But let me tell you my thoughts will all become some sort of
race

Hello ms popular, can you be my best friend
I want to kick you until you've reached your end

Send me to my room and I'll cry myself to sleep
Next day I'll get an A and my mind will keep running longer than
a day

One look in the mirror before I get in the shower
And my mind will crash like a leaning tower

Until I rejoice because I've starved myself for another hour

November 2014 (first poem I ever wrote)

The Mask You Wear

you can only wear a mask for so long
eventually, it just starts to feel so wrong
the mask will start to peel away
you can resist
try to tape it back
and make it stay
but it will persist
it will fall to the ground
leaving you there
to face who you really are
the mask you wear
will only get you so far

April 2019

Daddy, Dad, Father, Dead

I Think My Dad Loved Me?

He loved me
He loved me not
He loved me
Yes he did
Loved me so much
He couldn't hurt me
He wouldn't let himself
But he couldn't always stop himself
So instead he hurt himself
Killed himself
Thought it's better than hurting
His baby girl

November 2017

About My Dad...

I'm not trying to complain,
I usually smile through the pain,
but last night
I couldn't sleep
the moon was very bright
and my dad was on my mind
People tell me he was very kind
And maybe that doesn't apply to himself
But maybe if there wasn't a window in his room or he wasn't
given such a hard day, he still would have been here for my
16th birthday

June 2017

When My Dad Tried to Kidnap Me

Three of us hiding
Switching rooms, shutting windows
9-1-1 is called
He's looking in the windows
We're inside, can't be seen
Ducking down, hiding
Fear rushing in all of us
I know he'll take us
Mom would never let us go
Soon this will all be over

Tonight he will go
He will go to jail again
Because he wants us
Will put up a fight for us
But mom would never let that.

March 2016

Where Did Her Dad Go?

It could be that he's on a business trip
Maybe even at war
He sailed away and never washed up on the shore
Now I'll share the news
None of this is true
Nothing happened out of the blue
It may not be a fairytale
But it is very real
And it happens every day
It was never something
Anyone could have wished away
Sure, we tried and tried
Hoping we would make a change
Even though we never would
Truly waiting on a clock
Tick tock tick tock
All we do is stare
Nothing we do can help
I've already said my last prayer
So we wait for the call
To confirm he ended it all
We hear the ding
We hear the ring
We're not gonna answer
At least not today
We don't have to pick it up
To know he's gone away

July 2016

This poem is written as one of my interpretations from the
perspective of mostly my mom, but also my dad's family
(sisters, brother in law, parents, etc.) and people who knew him
in his life and had some awareness of his struggles and
situations.

I Choose

Someone I knew gave up and jumped. Period.
I chose to stay and keep on writing. I chose ;

March 2019

When Your Daddy Kills Himself

Well, he never really was my daddy. Maybe for a year at the most, but that's generous. In and out of my life, up and down in his own behaviors. My sister came along and things got worse for him. We left and hid from him. I don't exactly know what happened or why he chose death over trying, but he did. It's irreversible and non-negotiable. For a while, with my mom I only called him Steve. I guess it was weird to talk about my missing parental figure with my present parental figure without ending up in a rabbit hole of confusion and sorrow. With my dad's parents and sisters, I would refer to "my dad." They told me stories about the way he looked at me with such joy and marveled over our matching big brown eyes with a little mole under the right one, about how he used to carry his sister like a sack of potatoes and play with her throughout the house, or steal her cookie dough as she was baking. He ate poison ivy once, just because he was told not to. Got to watch out for that curiosity monster sometimes, huh? He hid in his sister's car on the way to her date, after he scared her, they went out for ice cream. He got tattoos of mine and my sister's names. He made up songs for me and my sister, mine went something like this, "run, run, run along, now we're gonna' sing the peanut song... wah, wah oh what a thrill, it finally was confirmed that peanut was a girl...". There was admiration and love. The love never disappeared, it more shifted, as I deeply love his family, his parents and sisters. They are no less my family than if my dad never died. In fact, they might even be more so now because over the years, their words have put together a picture of my dad, each story like a little puzzle piece. Now when I hear someone say "your dad" or "Steve" I see a moving man, someone with a loving smile and big brown eyes, a tall witty person who enjoyed nature and all the ladies in his life, me and my sister included. I don't see a dead man because I never saw a dead man. The stories I've heard are of a man who gave brand new gloves to a homeless quadriplegic man in the winter, a man who wrote love letters to his baby girls and brought laughter to every conversation. He abused my mom, no doubt, so I can't call him my daddy. A daddy shouldn't abuse your mommy who you love so dearly, so it's too much of a mindfuck to say "daddy." But he's not my "dead dad" or my "biological father." He's just my dad. Doesn't matter where he is anymore, his picture has been painted, his laughter has been heard and those will forever live in my heart.

March 2019

Where Was My Daddy Before?

The last time I saw my daddy was in a dream last year
My body shook and my heart raced
I got up and paced
Then slept on the floor
My mind was on repeat
"But where was my daddy before?"
He'll come back soon, I'm sure
Little me likes to believe, but
My dreams are tired of hoping
And in the daytime I'm tired of coping
Ya know
Wishes come and wishes go
I've never felt this way before
But I don't think I wish I had a daddy anymore

May 2019

Processing Death

I'll Cross the Bridge

I'll cross the bridge
I'll run or skip
I wonder who will be there
If it will feel like walking on air
Maybe we'll all hold hands
Maybe there will be some sort of dance
I bet there will be music
I bet there will be songs
I guess up there
There is no right and wrong
I will always know what to do
What to say
And what to pursue
I guess up there
There is no hate
I am quite excited about the irrelevance of
Who's good and who's great
One thing I want to know
Is how we will communicate
Maybe we'll talk
Maybe it will be in the way we walk
Maybe with our eyes
Or possibly
There will be no need
Because we will all perfectly harmonize

February 2017

The Story of Casper and Oli from My Point of View:

The following poem (Tick Tock) was written 2 nights after we had to put my sister's little 7-month-old kitty to sleep. We had adopted 2 cats, Casper and Oli. Casper was a royal, clean, soft little cat. Oli was a stray with messy fur and didn't know how to clean himself or use the litter box very well. Casper taught him. Casper showed Oli the ways of being a cat. He cleaned Oli until Oli learned for himself. Oli got cleaner, softer, and healthier. They both needed love, they both got that love. I would come home from school and sit on the couch with them for hours, they were so tiny that each of them would sit on one of my shoulders. I didn't have many friends at the time, but these kitties always made me feel less lonely and more loved. I would pet them for hours and that made me feel needed. All along, these were my sister's cats, she did everything for them. She bathed them, cleaned their litter box three times a day, vacuumed their kitty condo and even did work to help pay for their vet bills. As you can tell, they were her world. In December, Casper started acting weird, more aloof and he would hide a lot. We thought this might be because of all the Christmas decorations and music in our home. We later found out that he was very sick and had been getting worse each day, he had an extremely rare condition. As he got worse and could barely move or do much for himself, Oli would lie next him and clean him. Casper liked to be clean yet couldn't do that for himself, luckily, he had taught his brother, who was right there to comfort him in his last days. Me and my sister spent New Year's Eve singing and reading to Casper before she had to put him down the next day. Oli would go around the house looking for Casper and meowing in the spots he used to sit. We could tell he was sad, but he still seemed healthy. We gave him extra love and were thankful he was okay. A week after Casper's goodbye, Oli started acting out, doing naughty kitty things that he had never done before. We were frustrated until we took him to the vet and realized we were losing another kitty. He was put on morphine and we had to administer antibiotics to him in hopes of recovery, yet recovery never came. He was in immense pain his last few days and my sister knew he shouldn't have to "live" like that anymore. We took him to an emergency vet hospital and said our last goodbyes. He had caught the same incredibly rare disease that Casper had, as we learned that can be communicated when one cat cleans another. Casper taught Oli how to be a cat and for each of these short kitty lives, we are beyond grateful they were spent with us. We are grateful these kitties got to meet each other and become brothers and bless us with their cuteness every single day. The next poem, Tick Tock, was written mid-February, 2 weeks after Casper died and only 11 days before my sister's 14th birthday.

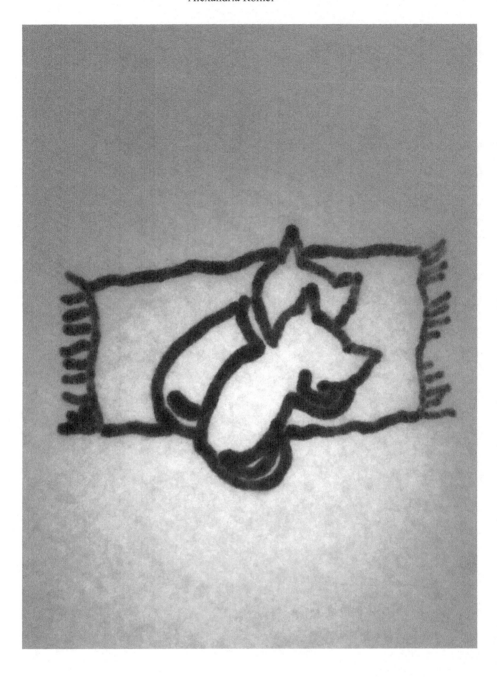

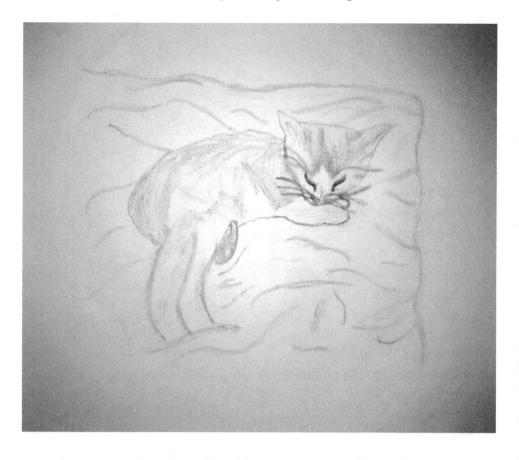

Alexandria Romei

Tick Tock

Tick tock
Tick tock
His life is on the clock
Don't cry
Don't die
Don't put up a fight
Right there he will lay
11 days before her birthday
Say goodbye
Say goodnight
Get ready to see the sunlight
It goes so quick
Just one little prick
It's not supposed to hurt
Sweetie you're alright
You're almost to the sunlight
Don't wiggle
Don't squirm
Please stay very still
It will help the dying liquid not leak out and spill
At this point we're only seconds away
Needle in one hand
His heart in the other
But soon they become one
And he's reunited with his brother

February 2017

The next poem, Hear Me Cry represents more processing on our kitties' death and death I've experienced in my own life and words I've heard and questioned as a kid…

Hear Me Cry

You say I'm alright
Honey you're okay
Don't put up a fight
But you're sending me back to where
It's sunny and bright

So was I okay
After I scraped my knee at the beach
Or were you sick of my struggling
Noises for speech

Please don't lie to me
When it comes to your words
You can't be so carefree

I'm very young and impressionable
And to tell you the truth
Your words are quite questionable

Don't tell me I'm alright
I'm not gonna die
Just because you don't want to hear me cry
Let me cry
I'll hear you sigh
But this is my last goodbye

February 2017

Alexandria Romei

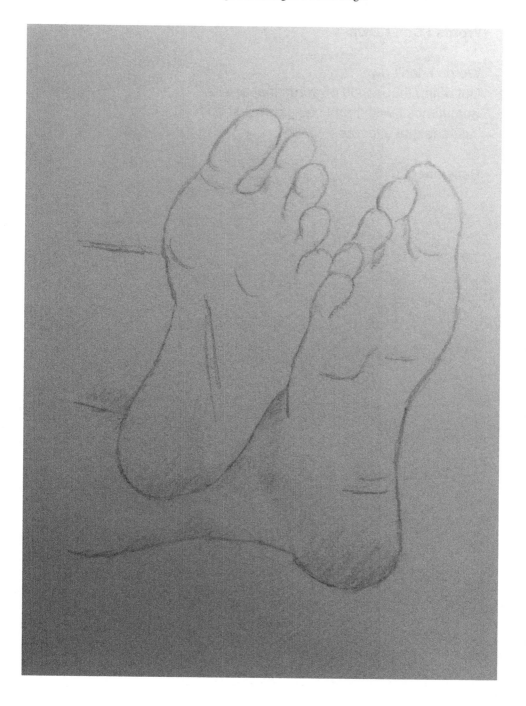

Words I Don't Own

Words I don't own
Out of the thousands of words that exist
Sometimes I wish that I could own just one
Just one that's for me

December 2018

I Walked the Blue, I Walked the Red

Listen
I know you'll be told
Blue is bad
And red is wrong
But green is the good way to go

If you go with green
Your life will be set
You will never be put to the test
You will be carrying around
A life-saving vest

But I will tell you
I walked the blue
I walked the red
I stepped on green
Once or twice
Only to find it
Wasn't so nice

As what they tell you

So please don't skip the blue
Or think you'll be dead
If you go with red

Get out of the box
And break the locks

Don't skip the blue
Because I fed the red
And to tell you the truth
I'm nowhere near dead

July 2016

Alexandria Romei

Where Do I Address My Prayers?

Can he hear me
Is he listening
Is he near me
Or up in the sky
I wonder if I've ever seen
One of his angels fly by
Maybe I've mistaken it for a cloud
I usually say my prayers out loud
I hope he knows what I say
I don't say them very loud
It's usually a whisper
At the very end of my day
I listen for him
For his voice
I know what I believe in
Just not which religion I fit in
It's a very big choice
To label yourself
With an entire religion
Some people think
To be Christian
And the Bible you read
Is purely fiction
But my intuition
Says the Bible is a source
Not the source
Sometimes religion
Can look like an addiction
When it's all somebody
Can talk about
And think about
And they dedicate their self to it
See, I know what I believe in

attention of everyone and the feedback I received was overwhelming. Adult poets praising me on my willingness to take risks and speak so vulnerably has continued to encourage my creativity. Afterward, the women in the bathroom told my mom she must be doing something right to have such a bold, outspoken daughter.

December 2018

The above poem was originally my UC school application short essay. Once I thought it was done, I had two problems. The first was that it was 392 words and my essay needed to be 350 or less. I had worked so hard to be as concise yet descriptive as possible. My goal was to tell this story in as few words as possible while making every word count. I went through each and every word of the essay, deleting what I could, but this is what I had left, and I wasn't going to edit it down anymore. After this realization, I received feedback that the whole thing was too poetic for a college essay, which needed to be more informative. Given these two hurdles, I decided these 392 words would be best for my poetry book, so I named the document "392 Word Poem", saved it on my computer, and then stayed up all night to rewrite my college essay.

The Gift to Sing

I can't really sing
I used to wish I could
But what a gift it is
To ask others to raise their voice
Against the strings of a guitar
Keys of a piano
Or beat of the drums
And share with the room
Their magical gift
Their words spill off their lips
The corners of their mouth have been raised
The room has become silent
Oh, what a gift it is

December 2017

Maybe I'm the Quiet One

My fan feels so loud
but maybe I'm the quiet one
the one with dreams who
never shares them
the one with aspirations who
never announces them
the wind can get so noisy
but maybe I'm the quiet one
the one with ideas who
never spreads them
the one with goals who
never chases them
screaming kids can push
your ears to their limits
but maybe I'm the quiet one
the one with manifestations who
never writes about them
the one with advice who
never lends it
ambulances can blast
your ears off
and that makes me feel
like the quiet one
but then I imagine
myself on a stage
WITH A VERY LOUD MICROPHONE
and one bright spotlight
shining right on me
my dreams and aspirations,
my ideas and goals
my advice and manifestations,
they all start to flood out
louder than my fan, louder than
the wind, and certainly louder
then the quickest red, flashing light- people saving vehicle

August 2018

The Best and the Worst Don't Want to Share

the best of me doesn't
want to share
and the worst of me
doesn't have any energy to care
the best of me wants all
of me
and the worst of me
wants none of me
they cannot meet
anywhere in between
as the best of me wants
things fair and square
but the worst of me
doesn't have empathy
to spare
somewhere in the
middle of all the tension
in the air
the worst of me
made a glare
right into the eyes of
the best of me
and the best of me
said "I'm kind"
I swear
to rid of you
I do not dare
the best of me
knows that
the worst of me
makes the best of me
stronger
oh, what a great pair
what lies in the
middle of the best

of me and the
worst of me
lies somewhere
between
over there and anywhere
but the worst of me
is getting tired
back to analyzing life
it speaks up to declare
after all this isn't a
questionnaire,
just a little poem
to share
that embracing the
best of yourself
and the perceived
worst of yourself
isn't a nightmare
it's actually an answer
to every single wish
or prayer

August 2018

Verbal Filter Glow up

I glow and I grow
everyday
a new way
when I was young
I had no filter
a slip of the tongue
too common
many things just came out
I would make a joke,
evoke laughter and smiles
but I never thought
before I spoke
sometimes my words caused
more harm than good
now speaking with a filter
is a bit more familiar
yet still, a few things
will slip out of my mouth
thought it never ends up as south
as it did before
it was clear that I grew
when I was about to say something
just a bit beyond woo-woo
but I stopped myself right there
it's better to keep that inside
I knew
as a kid I really
had no clue
what to do
when crazy ideas came about
that I wanted to share
until one day I learned how to
close my beak

I realized it's best
to think
before I open my mouth
and speak
without a blink
now I save my weird ideas, thoughts,
and words
for poems on paper
where I can edit and tweak
before I let them leak
I knew I was growing up
when having a filter
I was starting to seek
the words came to my mouth
but I kept them in my cheek
to later spill on the paper
before a major mistake
that would make
heads shake
and conversations break
now I'm seventeen, a bit older and wiser
than the days I would speak the words
best left
for poems on paper

April 2019

Now it's Romei

it used to be Clegg
but we were in danger
that's when I realized
the world had too much anger

when you're four
you shouldn't be lying on the floor,
crying to your mom
about everything that appears to be wrong

you should be out in the sun
not getting anything done.
simply being a kid

not noticing all the shit
the anger and the danger

now it's been changed to Romei
I write it on all my papers
and it rhymes with Ray

but there was a day
when it wasn't Romei,
it was Clegg

for that we were
in pain
but so soon,
waiting became too lame

so, we were on the run
which wasn't the most
fun

but now it's Romei,
and to me that's okay

July 2016

Re: Your father

He was supposed to be
The first man that you love
Instead, you will love no man
You like women instead
What a coincidence.

March 2019

Struggle with My Shape

The pain is real
I can't escape
This is my journey
It's my job to change my shape
It may be 10x harder for me
Than it is for the majority
But the pain is real,
Sometimes it's all I can feel
Yet, my Hope
It is not allowed to steal
I cover the longing with laughter and smiles
But deep down I fear each meal
For me, the pain is so real
Some don't think it's a big deal
But this is my reality
I don't feel comfortable
In my own body
And I won't just let it be
This is my reality
And the only one
Who's going to change it
Is me

March 2019

Searching for the Me I Used to Be

Searching, searching
1, 2, 3
I no longer feel like me
What is this misery
Why does it feel like home
So soft and warm in here
With all these midnight thoughts

Where did my own mind go?
What did I trade it for?
I want the light me back,
I cry to the earth that lays beneath the fabric of my pillowcase
I can't sleep like this
Not in this unfamiliar place…

The mind can race and race
All it wants
The body just won't doze off,
Won't surrender to peace and sleep
This weird new brain state, it would rather keep

But I can't live like this,
Not in someone else's brain
It's like forcing sunshine to look like rain

I stare at a reflection that I notice in the mirror
It captures my attention as I squint,
Look away, and then look again
I have…
My same body
How weird and unsettling
I still look like me
I guess.
Even in this foggy haze.

I don't know how many days
This has to last
But I want the *whole* me back
And that's all I ask

September 2018 & March 2019

Water, Waves, and Wonder

Dreams

My dreams
mostly feature
me, or
me being my personalities
at their extremes
I get to express every side of myself
that I don't express in the daylight

In my dreams,
my thoughts turn into beams
that spread over
the world around me

I lay down in the dark
to process my thoughts
and make room
for my wishes to
come true

I feel the whispers of the moon
on my eyelashes
as I drop in and out of
sleeping imagination

I feel the pitch black
on my skin
as I lay down for hours
to connect yesterday to tomorrow
and this is when I dream

February 2019

Dancing Underwater

I'm dancing underwater
my heart is getting hotter
as I open my eyes
to the rainbow coral
against the blue magic
of the open sea

my arms go up
as I twirl around
the citizens of the sea,
all the friendly fish,
kindly greet me

I dance through them
some are orange, some are brown
some are bigger than a car,
some don't even weigh a pound
there are babies and then
there are the wise ones,
the ones that wear an ocean crown
some are quiet,
some make quite the sound

I dance underwater
because I love seeing
1,000 different shades of
the color blue
on land, I only see a few
but in this ocean world,
I experience something new
unlimited colors
and beds made of seaweed
to make do

so that I can
lay on my back
and turn my eyes to
the place where
sun rays meet the ocean waves
daylight meets ocean wonder
and magic meets possibility

I lay on my bed of seaweed
taking in
this unheard of
world view

I pinch myself
yes, it's true
I'm dancing underwater
and even a dust of the magic I feel
is what I aspire my life
to live up to

dancing underwater,
I learn that the rainbow
is only a sneak preview
of what our eyes
are capable of observing

If only we take the possibility leap,
we get to dance in a new world,
something very few
will ever do
but if you go,
keep your eyes open
for every shade of magic ocean blue

February 2019

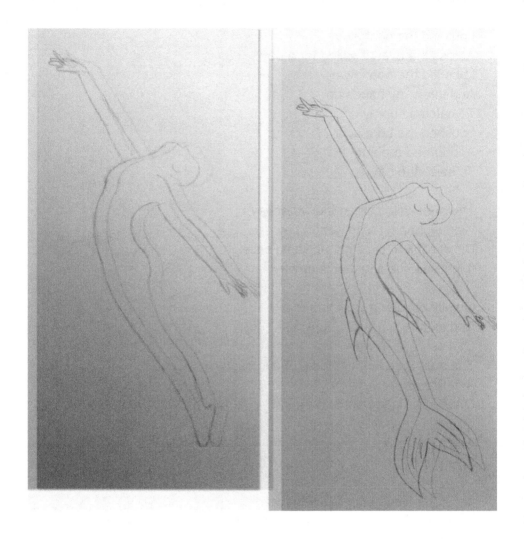

The Boat Sailed Across the Waterway

I pushed the boat away
Across the river, it sailed for a day
I pushed the boat away
And threw my hands up
To catch a sunray
I pushed the boat away
And turned around
To seize the day

The boat sailed along the waterway
Went right past a gorgeous bay
Didn't blink at the sight of Santa's sleigh
It just sailed along the waterway

Quietly passed a castaway
And didn't inquire the sight
Of a secret doorway
The boat lived in the middle of doomsday
And Broadway
Quietly shrugged at the mention
Of judgment day
And it wouldn't have fought back
If you said you were going to put it on display

It just... sailed along the waterway

March 2018

The Secret Doorway

The Secret Doorway
Lives behind a gorgeous bay,
Inviting and ready for children to run around it and play,
It offers as a lovely escape from the thoughts that can turn your
mind all gray

It lives under a lavender tree and between two bright green
bushes,
One that grows cherries
And the other, strawberries
If you lean your back against
This secret doorway
Your eyelids will kiss each other as you soak up
The magic of today
And let your mind twirl in the bliss
Of wonderment and everlasting play

A bit more about this secret doorway,
Its top handle is the color of when a glistening blue water beam
Meets a burning bright sun ray
And its bottom handle is
The color your cheeks turn
When you fall in love on a Monday

Behind an enchanting bay,
One that brushes your worries away,
There, lives the Secret Doorway

If your eyes ever fall upon it,
You'll feel a tingling rush of the married magic
From Valentine's Day and Santa's sleigh,
The gratitude on Mother's Day,
And a little bubba's smirk on their
First birthday (psst! make a wish here... yes, you! May your wish
come true <3)

Your hands will float up towards the sky
As you glide your fingers across
The ever-so captivating purple sunray

Then, you will rest your earthly body behind the Secret Doorway
And butterfly kiss your hands across the flowers to pray

If you look carefully through the peephole,
You'll see midnight blue sparkles
Twinkling in the air
From the nearby waterway

And if you ever forget where this is,
Just look for floating song lyrics
That lead you to a whimsical bay,
Gently brush past the singing leaves,
Open your eyes, then open them again
Pause and say "thank you"
And right there,
You will find
The Secret Doorway

March 2018 & March 2019

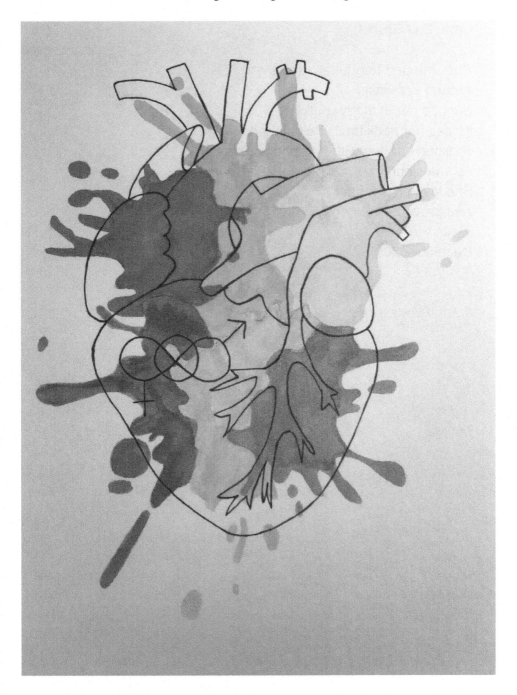

Little Luv Story

She wrapped her guitar strings
Around her wrists
Sang to her in the moonlight
Kissed her neck until she laughed
Brushed her hair with her long fingers
As she slept
She loved her for her
And proved it every day

December 2017

Higher Than This World

Concrete Jungle #1

There's this concrete jungle
I keep it in my head
So I have some place to store my thoughts
My flowers and my sharks live together in this concrete jungle
They fight like animals
Soft kittens and tigers fighting for food

November 2016

Concrete Jungle #2

I once thought up a jungle
then built it out of concrete

Now It lives in my head

This concrete jungle
It never sleeps
It never goes to bed
I keep it in my head

It thinks up new thoughts for me everyday

Some thoughts are new
Some thoughts are old
Some are nice
Some are rude
Some are angry
Some are loud
Some whisper
Some stomp

But they all live (and scream) in my head

November 2016

Don't Break the Ice

Not being good enough
Is like skating on a frozen pond
In the winter
Making perfect lines
With frozen blades
Staying light
So you don't break the ice
Only going over
The same line
In even numbers
Not leaving
Unbeautiful marks
Turning your mistakes
Into perfect 8's
You must be fragile
On the delicate ice
No slipping
No messing up
The game is over
When you've
Fallen down
Stay light
My dear
Stay perfect
My dear
Stay good enough
Don't break the ice

January 2017

Sometimes poems express themselves one way and then later you read it over and all the feelings that caused that poem come back, they come back so strongly that they practically insist on being expressed once again. That's what happened with this poem, Don't Break The Ice, and the next poem you will read, Not Being Good Enough was inspired from the former poem as well as the feelings it sparked in me over a year later when I read it again.

Not Being Good Enough

Not being good enough
Is never really about the being
rather always about the feeling:
I feel unworthy
I feel too heavy
I feel like I take more than my share in this world

Feeling unworthy
is like wondering if you should
get off the ice rink
so there's more room for others
it's like worrying that you might break the very ice you're skating
on
with the heaviness and burdens you're carrying
it's as if you're constantly torn between tearing yourself down
for not feeling more grateful
or for not being worth more

Feeling unworthy is a never-ending battle between criticism
and desire

I desire to be grateful and to love myself
but instead of a burning desire, it's a frozen desire
it's just… there, still, unmoving
it's visible, yet stagnant

I recognize the desire, yet I am helpless,
I feel too heavy and greedy to ever deserve
those warm emotions
so instead, I get used to the frozen ones
instead, I try to be "good enough"

But I'm not.
I will never be good enough for expectations that exceed
perfection.

Yet...
I still try,
which feels like skating on a frozen pond
in the middle of winter,
it's a beautiful idea
yet in reality, it takes delicacy

I'm skating, turning, twirling,
making perfect lines
with frozen blades
staying light
so I don't break the ice
only going over
the same lines
in even numbers
not leaving
unbeautiful marks
turning my mistakes
into perfect 8's
I must be fragile
on the pond's thin, winter ice
no slipping
no messing up
no making cracks
or falling down
I must balance on the blades
while creating visual perfection
I must try to be good enough
while dismissing my desire
for self-acceptance

I must stay light
so that I don't break the ice

April 2019

My Ghost is Gone

Your innocence is driving me crazy
I can't find my ghost anymore
Where did it go
What happened to the storm I used to possess
I'm finally sleeping now
I miss you sleeping next to me
What happened to your old soul
I'm searching for something I can't reach
I can't find my ghost anymore
And it's driving me crazy

November 2017

Mania

I'm stuck in this mania
It's wonderful up here
I can literally do anything
Don't bring me down
Way down
I could go
It's bright up here
Have you entered my mind?
I see the world in chrome
Your favorite Instagram filter
Is my eyesight home
But when I'm brought down
It's black and white
White and black
I can't get my mind back
Don't bring me down
It's lovely up here
Up in my manic mind

Heyo

I march to the beat of my own drums
welcome to the other side
where all that's high is yours and mine

You and Me

I think of you
I think of me
I think of what we could be
We'll name our kids after the stars
I'll count your freckles in the moonlight
Don't interrupt
This mania
I've never felt so deadly bright

All 3: December 2017

Our Song

Your song and my song
Sound so good together
Even those asleep
Could hear the moonlight
Smiling as our words
Combine in harmony
Against a melody
Don't press stop
We are at an all-time low
Arrived at the final destination
The feelings are piled upon my heart
We wrote the song together
Nothing can bring us apart

December 2017

One Last Day

I love airplanes
because I love to fly
I get kinda high

Due to the absence of anxiety
but the presence of variety

of people that were so close
to us, they meant the most

providing knowledge
now learned in history

what they can see of us is a mystery

I don't mean to be cliché

but what would you say
if you had one more day

with someone you once knew
just one catch
you can only speak what's true

because inside
the true and the untrue have part
the lies have died

You're left with the honest
and that is what you may say
when you get
your one last day

July 2016

I Look to the Stars for Answers

I look to the stars for answers
Sometimes I see mini-moon dancers
Twirling around in a galaxy of glistening lights
And midnight moon magic
My eyes widen, my breath slows
A feather floats across my back
A mantra presents itself as a whisper in the dark
My body floods with amazement
Butterflies prancing down my limbs
Fairies in the air around
My eyes get a bit wider, my breath a bit slower
I smile and sigh...
I can't believe this universe is ours

December 2017 & March 2019

Crazy

crazy is not just a phase
it is kind of a way of life
but not always
a way of living

April 2018

Burnt Disguise

Covered eyes
Burnt disguise
Tonight is an escape
From those dreary skies
And overused lies
We create for ourselves
To avoid emotional ties
To the evil goodness
That lies
Outside of you and me

May 2019

Alexandria Romei

Redemption

Dear Voice in My Head:

You tried to lock me away
You tried to make me stay

You told me I'd never succeed
You told me I'd never be freed

You tried to make me worthless
You told me I had no purpose

You thought I was breakable
You thought I was incapable

Of being inspirational,
Of taking all the aggression
All the pain, shame, and blame,
And using it as fuel

Finding my way out
And starting something new

Leaving behind
All the worthlessness with you

Now I'm
Breaking through the walls,
Running through the halls,
Reaching my lungs capacity
To share my story with the world,
To regain my freakin sanity
And find my own gravity

I'm now telling you that
You were wrong.

And you were weak.
You didn't break me,
You didn't stop me

Now I'm here,
Feeling confident and worthy
Saying loud and clear
That all the shit
You put me through

Only freakin empowered me
So, thank you.

April 2017 & April 2019

Shine on Me

Moonlight
Shine bright
God, I need you tonight
Jesus, can you hear me
Please set my mind free
I'm craving a visit
From one of your angels
God please tap into my soul
And release what's old
I'm craving something new
Something that can
Only be provided
By you
I know you have a plan
So, I will just
Send in my prayer
And put the rest in your hands
In your care
Life isn't always fair
But this is my message of faith to share

February 2018

Can't Call It Defeat

Four Walls
Black halls
Put up a fight
Got trapped all night
I tried to run
You stopped me
The screaming was fun
Until you nailed me down
Then put an intimidating amount of pressure on both of my shoulders
I gasped for breath
My throat had never felt so thin
Two options I was given
Cooperate
Or suffer
My mind went to a blank state
I couldn't think straight
But you wouldn't wait
I was willing to cooperate
It sounded better then
Letting this pain escalate
Unfortunately, I couldn't communicate
So, I lay there
Panting
Crying
Praying
You cuffed my hands
New scratches on my palms
You kicked my knees in
And forced me to my feet
Slammed me against the concrete
But I smiled
Because I was still alive
Which meant
My life was not yet complete
I had more hearts to touch
And more stories to share
Therefore, you can't call this defeat
Just bittersweet
If you will

March 2018

Just Tired

When I'm tired
I either turn to self-destruction
or creative construction
it just depends on
if I have yet
lost all mental function
sometimes I just
try
and I try
and I still
can't help but cry
sometimes I cry
cry for angels
for Jesus
for hope
but other times
I find myself begging for
someone to tie my neck with a rope
gosh, tiredness
is such a slippery slope
the other night
I wrote a
suicide note
but I didn't quite put it in the envelope
I am thankful to still be alive
I know someday
at Heavens door
I will arrive
but right now is not quite my time
right now
I am here
to not just
survive, but truly thrive
Thank you
angels

January 2018

Remember Me

I am thankful for this breath,
this gift of consciousness
and awareness
My past,
I will not be reliving
instead, the days
ahead of me
will be life-giving,
filled with a bit of crazy,
and a bit of smart
I hope to be remembered
not for my crazy
or my smart
but for my life- giving heart

April 2018 & February 2019

It Didn't End, So Here It Begins

Here I lay in a mental hospital
My thoughts shallow
And my bones brittle
The air thin
And my scaly skin
Sadness stored within
Tears held back
Background noise consists of a
"Worried whispers and offerings of juice" hospital noise
soundtrack
A new patient is coming in with an autistic meltdown
Another with an anxiety breakdown
Here I lay with a heart attack
As in my heart has slowly stopped working
And two days ago, it decided to…
Quit
As I looked down
I didn't even brace for it
I just weirdly held my breath
And Jumped
You could have heard my thump
Against the pointy rocks
And thorn bushes
Laying there to ensure my death…
At least I thought.
Yet here I am,
these doctors and nurses managed to save my breath.
I have come to understand that right here,
On this cold bed
Is where my life begins
My arms still red
And the gossip of my attempt has yet to spread
But here I am,

More than a billion times lucky
To have kept my head
You see, my mind is a masterpiece,
Brilliant in all of its ways.
But wouldn't you agree
That some of the most brilliant people have been
The craziest?
And crazy is not just a phase,
it is kind of a way of life,
but not always a way of living.
I am thankful for this breath
this gift of consciousness and awareness
My past I will not be reliving
Instead, the days ahead of me
will be life-giving,
filled with a bit of crazy,
and a bit of smart
I hope to be remembered
not for my crazy
or my smart
but for my life- giving heart

April 2018 & February 2019

I Send My Judgements down the River

Hello
This is me
And you do not
Know me
I know your words
Are out of ignorance
But they are
Starting to become
A regular occurrence
I will not get mad
Because I can
Still see
Your innocence
And trust me
I can tell
The difference
Between sarcasm
And an actual
Interest
In minimizing
Ignorance
I am here to share
Not to judge
Please be open
And let
Your beliefs budge
Let me know
If it's too much
To take in
I know exactly
Where you've been
It's not very comfortable
But we all

Have a place
To begin
Let's open
Our hearts
And look within
We will peel off
This artificial skin
The judgements
We hold
Let's release them
Down the river
I will let go
Of my grudges
For I am a
Forgiver
And the understanding
That I have
To you
I will deliver
Right now
I am a stranger
To your heart
But I am
Reaching out my hand
And asking for
A fresh start
My goal is
To take my judgements
And tear them apart
Please join me,
For this could be
A work of art

January 2018

Treasures to Re-Remember

The redness of the blood dripping down a new mother's thighs

The glowing orange in the sky singing Good Morning

The yellow traffic light reminding you to slow down sometimes, that life isn't always go, go, go, stop

The freshly cut green grass that feels like soft little forests beneath your bare toes

The deep blue of an ocean, larger than your thoughts can conceive

The twinkling purple that lays over the clouds like a blanket putting you to sleep continuously, every night, like a promise that can't be broken

The small glimpses of the purest treasures we've all been offered from day one, that we often skip over because we're so busy with our own lives that we almost forget about life

May 2017

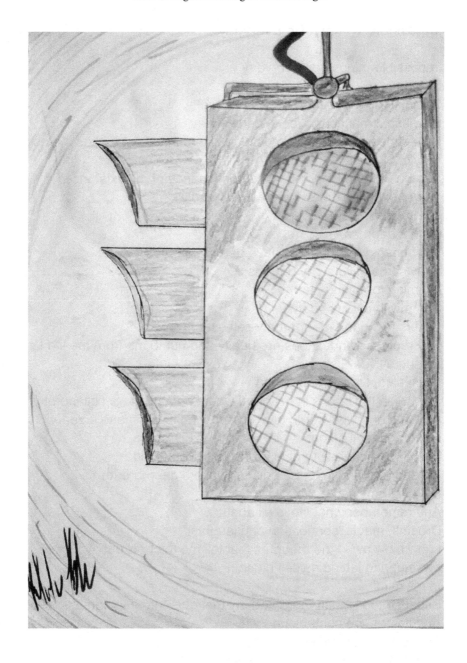

Impossible Things I Do Everyday

Impossible things I do everyday
Include
Standing up in the morning
Because it makes me feel a certain way
Sometimes dizzy, sometimes high, sometimes just makes me ask:
Why?
Getting out of bed signifies the continuance of my existence
And sometimes that's too much to handle
I promise
I'm not depressed
I just have questions that have been repressed
They come alive in my dreams
My mind forms into teams
Some with joyous beams
Others trying to tear apart my self esteem
The repressed questions are heavy and numb me from the life I'm
meant to live
Like I said, I'm not depressed
I just wish the teams in my head would be a bit more collaborative
And that one side would give up on trying to get me to scream,
shout and let it all out
Every day I choose to give power to the other side
Instead of giving in to the poison, I take a deep breath
Put aside my self-doubt
And remember what life is all about:
Dreams, magic, connection and laughter
I now blow away the thoughts that tell me to checkout
I've stopped letting myself hideout
In my mind
Because too long in there and my thoughts turn into flames
And flames are contagious
So instead I remain courageous
And do things every day I once saw as impossible

December 2018

Run Faster Towards the Life You're Running For

Run run
Run away
Go chase the next day
What's in store
Will go away
If you don't run
Faster
Faster
Catch it
Quickly
You're in a hurry
Catch the moment
You're waiting for
You're here
Right now
But that, you can ignore
You're never present, sure
But there's a moment
You're chasing
So run, run
Run along
Quicker
Quicker
Until maybe you
Realize
The moment is now
And hopefully
You can live it a little
Before you forever
Close your eyes

May 2019

Loss Comes in Many Forms

The Earth Is Dying and My Great, Great Grandchildren Are Crying

When you heard
The birds die
And the children cry
The president lie
And the enemy's words pass by
Great, great mama,
What did you do?
When the sky
Was no longer blue
And you were getting sicker too

When Hurricane Harvey Was through
Great, great mama
What did you do?
Did you have to see all
The fishes choke
Or was it when you
Witnessed the smoke
Is that finally when
You awoke?

Great, great mama,
Where moving to Mars
We will no longer get
To live in the house
That was once ours
I have to leave behind
Everything of mine
Including pictures of you

Great, great mama,
If you knew that,
What would you do?

September 2017

The War Line

One
Two
Three
Four
March down the line
We're all going to war
One
Two
Three
Four
Five
Right now is not the time to be alive
One
We stand straight
Two
We prepare the triggers
Three
We will now shoot you
Four
You will shoot us next
Five
This is called orderly fashion
Six
It requires our brothers and sisters to put their lives on the line
Seven
This is called orderly fashion
When we all stand in line
And take our turns to die

September 2017

Baby Hat

Baby hat
Mama sewed the baby hat
Daddy worked two shifts
They ended up with a baby hat
And money to pay the rent

November 2017

Privilege

To me
Your worst nightmare
Sounds like a bedtime story
My dear, you have nothing to fear
Your life is nowhere near
The way I live everyday
You'll fear what you fear
And that's okay
You don't know it
Any other way
But please just be grateful
For what you have in this world
That so many others
Would be beyond grateful
To own and to hold

May 2019

Illumination

I Am Here

Don't bother trying to disrupt me
Or make me want to go
I am in my flow
I am here
I've already seen the bottom
So there's nothing to fear
I know that I'll be ready when the devil is near

April 2019

To Be in the Light

To be in the light
The happy
The joy
Is to have been through dark
And marched yourself through
The heartbreaks
The deaths
The tantrums
The pitch-black nights
The scars
The suicide attempts
The beaten rope
The exes
The ones you loved
The ones you still love, but lost
The emotions that have no name
The emotions that have too many names
The feelings that feel too much
The feelings that don't feel enough
The words that won't come out
The hands you'll never get to hold
The broken glass
And the evilness
Through this you will know the light
The shining light
The sunshine
The smiles
The love
The joy

December 2017

Yoga

There's this little place that people go
They always leave with a smile to show
There's this little place that people go
Their hearts beat fast and their hearts beat slow
Their hearts beat fast and their hearts beat slow
There's this little place that people go
When their moods are high and when their moods are low
There's this little place that people go
What this place is
I do not know
They speak of movement
And they speak of flow
They place their hands to their hearts
And watch the world unfold
They become airplanes and moons
Triangles and lizards
There's this little place that people go
Where they learn to touch left ear to their right toe
There's this little place that people go
They believe in earth and love and ground and sky
They let their love fly high
Oh, off to this place I shall go

June 2018

Young Girls Will Change the World

Young girls will change the world
Let's just give them space and time, for true hearts need
lightness to shine
Not all girls have been given the best advice and I will tell you
that for that, society sure pays the price
Young girls are smart and strong so let us give them the tools
for their messages to be heard far and long
Young girls have brilliant hearts and personalities with many
parts
Let us recognize each one for what she can become
Let's empower each and every girl for the superwoman that
she is

Cisgender or trans, black, white, or tan let's give them all the
tools and verbal space that we can
Each message they gather the courage to share is to be seen
as a gift of truth and young wisdom
Their brains are still playdo so let's plant many seeds to grow,

let's instill the thirst for knowledge and the love of learning in each young girl

Listen up because to run like a girl is to sprint into the wind and to think like a girl is to foster your own creativity without letting any negativity in, let's ensure this message whether they are 5, 18 or ten, each of their young hearts deserves the sight of their gifts to be let in

My mission is to empower young girls. Your daughters, nieces and sisters are bound to change the world. Girls come in every color and size, each one deserves the encouragement to rise. Do not ever let shyness fool you, for the quietest speakers and the loudest listeners and the most observational watchers. They will mirror your actions to the exponent. Let us make that a good thing. Let us set the example of love and courage. We shall teach young girls to dare greatly and make leaps and bounds across platforms at the pace their heart desires. Young girls are the fuel to stop our hate fires.

Let's show them that it way always a cape, never a dress. Society has hushed many young girls' voices, we must confess. There is no tomorrow, there is only today and then the next today. There is only today to wrap them in their capes and show them their wings. Let them seize the day. Let them show us the way. Empower young girls.

June 2018

The World Is at My Fingertips

The world is at my fingertips
I will not stay Stagnant
Call me what you will
But this is my emotional eclipse
The sun is my source of illumination
Her rays are my scripts, my caption, my passion
My mind's negativity is experiencing deflation
This is an act of liberation
The world is at my fingertips,
And the words: yay, yikes, ouch, and ahh are
Living right in front of my lips
My imaginative thoughts have turned into spaceships
And the world is at my fingertips
I wake up next to the ocean shores
Just to hear the ocean roars
I ask for opportunities
And the universe opens doors
I sit there and watch the waves
The water goes down and as it dips,
I realize that the world has always been at my fingertips

April 2018

Alexandria Romei

To Fly

To jump is to exert effort,
To *try,*
To force this body off the ground

To Fly is to let go
To *not* try,
To let this body float into the air,
And then surrender as you twirl around in the bliss up there

March 2019

A World of Connotations

I live in a world of connotations
Where women and weak
Are synonyms
Where baby boy
Means bright future
And little girl
Means five toys for boys
Two right at their convenience when having a conversation
And two more at their convenience

When you've turned around

They are just so distracting
You may not show the straps or laces
That cover them up
Because "boys will be boys"
They will make boob jokes
And rate girls' asses
It's just in their nature
Like they were born with sexualizing glasses

You have the sex
If they pay the taxes

But unfortunately
One little toy
Is a bit more hidden

That's were consent
Comes in

Because eye candy
Is perfectly free

But physical pleasure
Is thought of as a treasure

That if you somehow capture,
It's yours to keep

I'm so sorry boys
That pussies are harder to get to

That you have to dig for them
Hold us down for them
Shut us up for them

And I deeply apologize
That sometimes
In the midst of doing all this

You forget to
Ask for
Consent for them

July 2016

I wrote this poem just after I turned 15 years old. I was really discovering my voice at this time, which expressed itself both through writing this poem and then reading it loud at an open mic night in Greenwich Village, on my first trip ever to NYC.

I Like the Stars

You can't like the stars
You have to like the moon

Stars will always be there
They will always have a purpose
But you can't like them

If you like the stars
You go away

If you like the moon
You stay

You can always lie
Because if you like the stars
That's the only way to get by

Now imagine this
You can't like the moon
You can only like the stars

If you say you like the moon
People will laugh
People will stare

Then you will realize that
Only being allowed to like the moon isn't fair

July 2016

Not Sure Which World I'm Living in

I keep switching worlds
Not sure which one is my reality
So much numbness
So much anxiety
I keep on reliving my own fatality
Where's the life I want to live
Come on, I'm ready
I used to be so surface level
So artificial
Cup half full
Typa girl
Now this cup is overflowing
Overwhelming
Like a waterfall
Too wide and too tall
You want to touch it
But you know you'd fall
Right in and there'd
Be no one to call
No one who's really there for you
Reality keeps switching back and forth
Black
And then blue
Purple
Gray
And sometimes all the color just fades away
Everyday I'm living in
Fight or flight or cry and try
Once again
It's the cycle I feel so stuck in
I'm not sure when
It all will end
When the numbness will begin

But maybe it will not
Maybe sticking this out is worth a shot
There may be something better
On the other side
Something better than the happiness
I've so far experienced
Maybe after this is over
The old me will have died
And the new me will be rising
Rising, and rising
With my heart resizing
I guess
These overwhelming feelings
Come as less surprising
If I'm aware of the transformation
Arising
In my spirit
My soul
My being
My non-human self
...
Thank goodness
Because after all this truth
I feel as if I can
Now breathe and surrender into it

July 2019

Out of Madness Comes Treasure

I burst with creativity
Moving from reality to reality
Do I ever stay in one place?
Not really
Shifting gears
Facing fears
Shedding tears
And blasting mirrors
Poem after poem
The words just flow in
And then glue to the paper
What's up with her, they ask?
Oh, she lives in her own world
We just let it be
So that we can read
Her poetry

May 2019

Illustration Credit:

Sophia Romei- drawing for "Humans. Create. Poetry.", drawing for "The World is at My Fingertips", drawing for "Slingshot", drawing for "I Want to Walk Without Shoes Today", drawing for "I Chose", drawing for "Our Song", drawing for "I'll try to Practice What I Preach", drawing for "Love: Short Poems", drawing for "Dancing Underwater", drawing for "Unfair Systems", drawing for "Searching For the Me I Used To Be", drawing for "Water, Waves, and Wonder" section title page, drawing for "Fix Me with Meds", drawing for "I Like the Stars", drawing for "Whichever Way For You", drawing of a beaming red heart, drawing of a forest/ teacup

Rebekah Blazer- drawing for "My Ghost is Gone", drawing for "Searching for The Me I Used To Be", both drawings for "Her baby hands will heal me", drawing of a lavender colored tree, drawing of traffic lights, drawing of a hospital room

Evelyn Thom- drawing of a pair of ice skates

Katie Blair- drawing for "Flower with Power"

Avlynne Johnson- girl blowing bubbles

Addy Johnson- rainbow colored heart

Kynlee Johnson- two red hearts

Alexandria Romei- (Author) drawing for "Wounded Hearts", all three drawings for "The Story of Casper and Oli"

A huge Thank YOU to Sophia Romei and Rebekah Blazer for contributing so many amazing drawings and for doing them specifically for certain poems. It really amazes me what you each came up with and I am so grateful to have your artwork in my first book.

Made in the
USA
Monee, IL